21st Century Junior Library

Maiasaura

by Jennifer Zeiger

CHERRY LAKE PUBLISHING * ANN ARBOR, MICHIGAN

CHERRY LAKE
Publishing

Published in the United States of America by Cherry Lake Publishing
Ann Arbor, Michigan
www.cherrylakepublishing.com

Content Adviser: Gregory M. Erickson, PhD, Dinosaur Paleontologist, Department of Biological
Science, Florida State University, Tallahassee, Florida

Reading Adviser: Marla Conn, ReadAbility, Inc.

Photo Credits: Cover and pages 4 and 6, ©Mengzhang/Dreamstime.com; pages 8 and 20,
©MERVYN REES/Alamy; page 10, ©dieKleinert/Alamy; page 12, ©mikeledray/Shutterstock, Inc.;
page 14, ©Kevin Schafer/Alamy; page 16, ©Kostyantyn Ivanyshen/Shutterstock, Inc.; page 18,
©PRISMA ARCHIVO/Alamy.

LIBRARY OF CONGRESS CATALOGING-IN-PUBLICATION DATA
Zeiger, Jennifer.
  Maiasaura/by Jennifer Zeiger.
    pages cm.—(Dinosaurs)
  Includes bibliographical references and index.
  ISBN 978-1-62431-163-5 (lib. bdg.)—ISBN 978-1-62431-295-3 (pbk.)—
ISBN 978-1-62431-229-8 (e-book)
  1. Maiasaura—Juvenile literature. 2. Dinosaurs—Juvenile literature. I. Title.
  QE862.O65Z45 2014
  567.914—dc23   2013006492

Cherry Lake Publishing would like to acknowledge the work of
The Partnership for 21st Century Skills.
Please visit www.p21.org for more information.

Printed in the United States of America
Corporate Graphics Inc.
July 2013
CLFA13

CONTENTS

Baby *Maiasaura* were too small and weak to take care of themselves.

What Was Maiasaura?

A dozen tiny baby dinosaurs sit in a nest. Other young dinosaurs make sounds in their own nests nearby. Suddenly, the babies spot a huge dinosaur walking toward them. Its head alone is larger than a baby's entire body! The giant dinosaur leans over the nest with its mouth full of berries. The babies hungrily eat the food their parent has brought.

Adult *Maiasaura* were much bigger than their young.

These dinosaurs are called *Maiasaura*. The name means "good mother lizard." *Maiasaura* lived about 74 million years ago. They lived where Montana is today. But there are no *Maiasaura* living today. Like all dinosaurs, they are **extinct**.

Ask Questions!

How do scientists know what dinosaurs looked like? How do they know a dinosaur's shape? How do they know how much it weighed? Can scientists know a dinosaur's coloring? A teacher, librarian, or museum worker can help you answer these questions.

The shape of *Maiasaura*'s beak made it easy for the dinosaur to grab plants to eat.

What Did *Maiasaura* Look Like?

Maiasaura had a long snout with a flat **beak** at the end. Scientists sometimes call this beak a duck bill. It was sharp and toothless. The dinosaur's mouth was full of teeth. The teeth were wide and flat. This made them good for chewing leaves and berries.

Maiasaura could rise up on its back legs when it needed to.

Maiasaura usually walked on four legs. Its front legs were shorter than its back legs. Sometimes it stood up on its back legs. This helped it reach leaves and other food high in trees. *Maiasaura* had a long tail. This helped it **balance** when walking or running.

Maiasaura and other duck-billed dinosaurs had three toes on each back foot, leaving footprints like this one.

Maiasaura was very big. It could be 30 feet (9 meters) long from head to tail. It was about 10 feet (3 m) tall when it stood on all fours. It weighed as much as 3 tons (2,700 kilograms). This is about the same weight as an elephant.

Maiasaura was surrounded by possible food sources, such as the tree this fossil cone came from.

How Did *Maiasaura* Live?

Leaves and other plant parts formed *Maiasaura's* **diet**. *Maiasaura* used its sharp beak to cut off plant pieces. It chewed the food with its flat teeth. *Maiasaura* spent most of its days eating. It needed a lot of food to survive.

Tyrannosaurs were a predator of *Maiasaura*.

Hungry **predators** such as tyrannosaurs hunted *Maiasaura*. *Maiasaura* found safety in numbers. Sometimes thousands of *Maiasaura* gathered together. These dinosaurs could also run away from predators.

Make a Guess!

Maiasaura had flat teeth for chewing plants. But tyrannosaurs and other predators hunted and ate meat. Can you guess what kind of teeth these dinosaurs had? A teacher or librarian can help you find the answer.

Sometimes hundreds of *Maiasaura* nests were built in the same area.

Maiasaura was a good parent. *Maiasaura* built nests for its eggs. Hundreds of *Maiasaura* nests were built near one another. Babies could not walk when they hatched. Their parents brought them food until they grew big enough to feed themselves.

Fossils of adult and young *Maiasaura* have provided scientists with a lot of information.

Scientists learn about *Maiasaura* by looking at **fossils**. Fossils of young and adult *Maiasaura* have been found in Montana. So many egg fossils were found in one area that scientists call it Egg Mountain. These fossils taught scientists how *Maiasaura* cared for their young. There is still plenty to learn about *Maiasaura*. Will you make discoveries one day?

GLOSSARY

balance (BAL-unts) steadiness, the ability to stay up without falling

beak (BEEK) the horny, pointed jaw of a bird or other animal

diet (DYE-it) the food an animal typically eats

extinct (ik-STINGKT) describing a type of plant or animal that has completely died out

fossils (FAH-suhlz) the preserved remains of living things from thousands or millions of years ago

predators (PRED-uh-turz) animals that live by hunting other animals for food

FIND OUT MORE

BOOKS

Dixon, Dougal. *Maiasaura and Other Dinosaurs of the Midwest*. Minneapolis: Picture Window Books, 2007.

Gray, Susan Heinrichs. *Maiasaura*. Mankato, MN: Child's World, 2010.

WEB SITES

Animal Planet—Maiasaura
http://animals.howstuffworks.com /dinosaurs/maiasaura.htm
Learn more about *Maiasaura*, and check out links to images and information about other dinosaurs living at the time.

Dinosphere at the Children's Museum of Indianapolis—Maiasaura
www.childrensmuseum.org /themuseum/dinosphere/profiles /maia.html
Look at pictures and read more about *Maiasaura* and its discovery.

INDEX

ABOUT THE AUTHOR

Jennifer Zeiger lives in Chicago, Illinois. She writes and edits children's books on all sorts of topics.